PRAISE FOR *THE FIVE DEADLY SINS*

"If you're a creative person, it would be a sin to not read this book. *The Five Deadly Sins* gives you everything you need to sell your ideas and make them happen in the world."

—**Rob Schwartz**, Chief Executive Officer, TBWA\Chiat\Day

"You can't write a book like this unless you've been through the fire. Feuerman's frontline experience selling creative work comes through on every page."

—**Wilson Mateos**, Executive Creative Director,
Leo Burnett Tailor Made, São Paulo

"Agency creatives: cover your ears! A great idea is only 20 percent of the process. The other 80 percent is about convincing the client. Kerry's book is a must-read for serious idea-smiths."

—**Libby Brockhoff & Franklin Tipton**, Founders, Odysseus Arms

"Kerry Feuerman's insights are incredibly helpful for anyone making a presentation—creatives, account people, planners, clients—*anyone!*"

—**Stacy Milrany**, Creative Director, REI

THE FIVE DEADLY SINS

OF PRESENTING CREATIVE WORK

THE FIVE DEADLY SINS

OF PRESENTING CREATIVE WORK

KERRY Z. FEUERMAN

Published by Last Hurdle, Irvington, VA
lasthurdle.net

Edited and Designed by Girl Friday Productions
www.girlfridayproductions.com

Editorial: Emilie Sandoz-Voyer, Kirsten Colton, and Erica Avedikian
Interior and cover design: Paul Barrett
Cover and interior illustrations: Whitney Huhmann

ISBN (Paperback): 978-0-9997053-0-8
e-ISBN: 978-0-9997053-1-5

First Edition

Printed in the United States of America

With thanks—

When you spend a career telling entire stories in thirty seconds, writing a book—even a short book—can be an intimidating task. Special thanks to the trusted few who helped me through it: Bill Westbrook, Roger Feuerman, Karen Feuerman, and Sheri Lawson.

For Karen, my favorite.

CONTENTS

In 600 AD, Pope Gregory proclaimed there were seven deadly sins: Lust, Gluttony, Greed, Sloth, Wrath, Envy, and Pride. Had His Holiness run an advertising agency at the time, he would no doubt have included five more sins: Blurting, Ad Whispering, Wanderlust, Telepathy, and Impalement. These sins have killed more good creative ideas than all chief marketing officers combined.

CONFESSION

Clueless. That's how I'd describe myself early in my career. I had absolutely no understanding of what it took to sell creative work, no appreciation for the approval gauntlet that concepts had to run just to stay alive. All I thought about—and frankly, all I cared about—was doing the best work I could. I figured good work would sell itself. Like I said, clueless.

I remember coming back from a client meeting one day, dragging a portfolio full of unsold work into the agency, and telling my creative director, "The client is an idiot. He wouldn't know good work if it bit him in the ass. We should resign the account." The CD sat back in his chair, took off his glasses, and rubbed the bridge of his nose as if I'd just given him a headache. "What did you do to sell the work?" he asked.

"I presented it," I replied.

"No, that's not what I asked. What did you do to *sell* the work?"

Anyone can present creative work. Just show it. Sometimes that's all it takes to close the deal. But when it's not, which is most of the time, you better have a few more skills up your sleeve. Nobody's going to love your idea as much as you do unless you *make* them love it. Which means you have to think like a salesperson as well as a creative person. Winning hearts begins with winning minds.

I suggest you start by learning from my mistakes, or what I call the "five deadly sins." These are the things that reduce your chances of selling creative ideas, be they traditional, digital, social, UX, design, content, or anything else. I learned all five sins the hard, slow way: falling on my face, getting up, falling on my face again, getting up again. My goal in the following chapters is to help you avoid a similar level of bloodshed. Actually, it's more than that. I want to give you the foundation to become a *great* presenter. Great presenters are always bigger than the work. They approach a presentation holistically, considering the wants and needs of their audience above all else. In the real world of selling creativity to a bunch of hard-nosed business people, great presenters are like prosecutors in a courtroom: they know what they want the jury to think and then build a persuasive case for getting them there.

Great presenters
are always bigger
than the work.

So much of what we do in advertising—or any other creatively driven business, for that matter—is out of our hands. We can't control dead-lines, budgets, or the approval process. But when you're presenting in front of a roomful of people, it's *all* in your hands. For those brief few minutes, you can orchestrate the situation any way you want. You can set the mood and energy level of the room, shape opinions, get heads nodding, make smiles appear. If you know what to do with them, pre-sentation skills are *power*; they shift control in the room to you. How you use that power to keep your ideas alive is the sole purpose of this book.

In fact, let's not even call it a book. It's a survival guide. If you were stranded on a desert island, you'd be glad you read *How to Stay Alive on a Desert Island*. Same goes for being in a presentation, surrounded by all the dangers that can mortally wound brilliant ideas. Knowing how to identify, preempt, circumvent, and defend against these dan-gers is often the difference between work dying and work surviving. But before you turn the page, know this: there is no silver bullet. No single thing that by itself is guaranteed to sell more work. The best presenters use multiple tools to make incremental gains here and there, which add up over the course of a presentation and hopefully result in a green light for production. You may never know which tools worked and which didn't. That's why you need to arm yourself with as many as you can.

Or maybe the work will just sell itself.

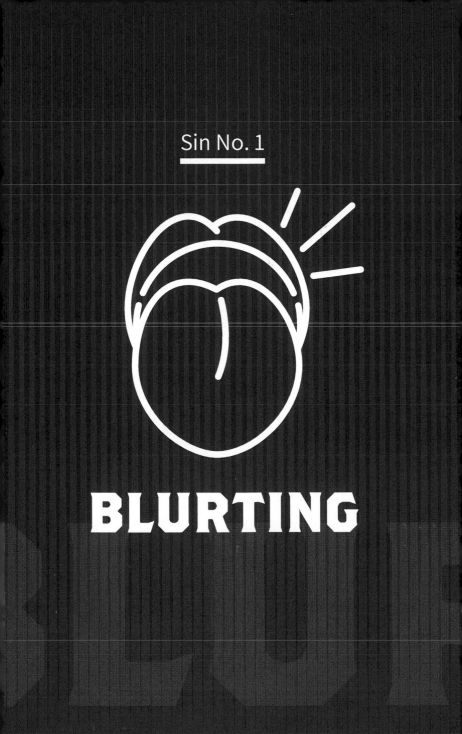

Sin No. 1

BLURTING

✚

If someone put a gun to my head and told me to choose the worst sin to commit, I'd know the answer immediately. Hopefully that will never happen, but if it did, my response would be Blurting: the deadliest sin of all.

Blurting is when you leap into presenting an idea with absolutely no preamble whatsoever. The first words out of your mouth are "We open on. . . ." There's nothing about how you approached the assignment. No mention of the problem you're trying to solve. You so badly want to sell your idea that you completely leave out the reasons why it's worth buying.

Great presenters never show work totally naked, that is, without some sort of setup. It doesn't have to be long and drawn out, but it does need to be smart. The goal is to predispose your audience to want to buy the work *before* you ever show it, which means it has to sound like a solution to the client's business problem, not just a cool idea. I call this "Why Before What."

Why Before What requires you to do a little homework before the presentation.

1. **Know what the client is trying to achieve (the business goal).**
2. **Study the creative brief, especially the target audience and strategy sections.**
3. **Find the connective tissue between one and two and the creative ideas you're going to present.**

Then make your setup interesting, compelling, entertaining—*anything* but a boring regurgitation of the assignment.

Think of it like this: two parallel lines, one above the other. The top line represents the client's business goal. The bottom line is your creative work. Unless you flunked ninth-grade geometry, you know that parallel lines never intersect, which is how bad presenters show work. Good presenters, on the other hand, use some form of Why Before What to turn parallel lines into intersecting lines. And for a client, that's where the love is.

fig. 1

FRAME THE WORK

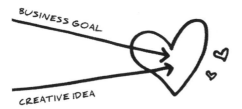

Presenters who make the lines intersect are more likely to have clients love their ideas.

Here's an example of a Blurting presenter versus a Non-Blurting presenter.

SITUATION: Business at your client's pizza chain is down, and the CMO wants an idea to spike sales immediately. The creative brief calls for a stunt to grab consumers' attention, followed by a five-dollar-off coupon on all large pizzas. Your creative idea is to have a monkey interview people on the street to see if they want five dollars off their next pizza.

BLURTER: "Good morning. Imagine you're on a street corner and a monkey with a microphone walks up and asks if you want five bucks off a large pizza. He holds up the mic to get your answer. We video your reaction and post it on social media . . ."

NON-BLURTER: "Good morning. A stunt is a tricky thing, a balancing act, really. If you don't go far enough, it can fall flat. If you go too far, the gag can overshadow the offer, and you end up not selling much of anything. One of the greatest stunts of all time, Burger King's Whopper Freakout, was a perfect balance between shocking and selling. By faking the discontinuation of the Whopper, BK created more desire. As a result, Whopper sales jumped significantly. So how can we do the same thing for your pizzas? Well, the first thing we need is a monkey. Imagine you're on a street corner ..."

Even the monkey knows which presenter was more persuasive. In less than thirty seconds, the Non-Blurter demonstrated a clear knowledge of the client's sales issue and gave valuable insight into the nature of stunts—*before* showing the idea. She was a creative person solving a business problem, turning parallel lines into intersecting lines. Even if the Blurter was as entertaining as hell, he was never going to match the level of confidence instilled in the client's mind by the Non-Blurter, who preceded her equally entertaining presentation of the monkey stunt with a little bit of smarts.

There's another downside to Blurting. It's called human nature. Quite often you'll be presenting to people who've never met you before. They're not familiar with the tone of your voice, your speech patterns, your personality—they know nothing about you. You're just a generic delivery person of creative ideas. Blurting gives your audience no time to get comfortable with you. No time to decide if they like you or respect you, never mind want to buy work from you. It would be like not shaking someone's hand and expecting them to immediately become your friend—a friend who's willing to give you a million bucks to produce a campaign! Good luck with that.

After fifteen years of study, Harvard Business School psychologists found that within the first minute of meeting someone new, people pass judgment on two things more than anything else: whether they trust the person and whether they think that person is competent, in that order. If you just walk into a room and blurt out an idea with no lead-in, your chances of establishing trust or competency go down, as does the likelihood of selling the work.

Case in point: When I was a creative director in Richmond, Virginia, I brought an art director to a client meeting. He was a very funny, likable guy, and I wanted him to meet the clients and present two humorous campaigns. After a quick hello I handed the presentation over to the art director. The very first thing he did was pull out a storyboard and start going through the spot. It was a classic case of Blurting, one that left the clients politely smiling but a bit underwhelmed. Then lunch was delivered. As everyone ate we talked about this and that, nonbusiness stuff, mostly. Somehow the art director began telling a story that had everyone laughing to the point of tears. I don't remember exactly what the story was about, but I distinctly recall it dramatically changed his relationship with the clients. Now they knew him a little better—liked him, even. After lunch he presented a second campaign, and it was approved on the spot. Was it better than the first work he showed? Not at all. Did the clients now *trust* him with part of their advertising budget and believe he was *competent* at producing humorous, engaging spots? Absolutely. Without that short bit of bonding during lunch, we could easily have gone back to the agency for a weekend's worth of reconcepting. As a presenter, *everything* matters.

A lot of creative people commit the sin of Blurting simply because they think the planner and account person have already done the setup. To a degree, that's probably true. But my guess is that it's more of a strategy setup than an actual setup of the work. Besides, let's say you've got three campaigns to show. There's no way an account person or planner can lay the groundwork for how each campaign answers the brief differently and effectively. That's the job of the person who is most familiar with the work, namely you, the presenter. If you're smart, you'll use the creative brief to your advantage, early and often. The last thing a client is expecting is a creative person to whip out the brief and actually talk about the assignment. (CUT TO INSIDE CLIENT'S HEAD: *Huh, I thought creatives ignored briefs.*) Instantly, you'll go from being a creative person in their eyes to an *advertising* person: a problem solver, business grower.

Within every creative brief there are several different launchpads for getting into the work: target audience, product benefits, competitive

The last thing a client is expecting is a creative person to whip out the brief and actually talk about the assignment.

situation, strategy, assignment, consumer insight, and so on. I've even used mandatories as my jumping-off point. Pick one of the launchpads and highlight it on the brief so it clearly stands out from everything else. Then use it to establish Why Before What. Pick a different one for each campaign. Not only does this create context for the work, but it helps clients separate and catalog all of the campaigns in their heads. If you return to the brief between campaigns, the work is less likely to blur together and cause confusion. Or worse, tempt the clients to mix part of one campaign with part of another. Not that they would do that, of course.

Before we move on from the sin of Blurting, I owe you a word of caution about setups. Every audience you present to—creative director, planner, account person, client—judges the work through a slightly different lens. And since they're all human, they also have different attention spans and levels of patience, from "tell me more" to "just show me the damn ad!" Smart presenters adjust the length of their setup based on who they're talking to and how much time they have. Given the pace of today's world, I'm often asked if I can just give an elevator-pitch version of the presentation. To which I respond, "What floor are we going to?" It's usually the second! The good news is, I've already planned for that possibility. I always figure out the most important thing to say before showing the creative work. I get it down to one or two very brief points and say them before anyone can stop me.

Here's an example of how I'd do an abbreviated setup. It's based on a real (brilliant) creative execution produced by an agency in Chicago. Since I didn't work at the agency, I have no idea what the creative brief said, so I'm going to make it up.

IMAGINARY BRIEF: The client is a company that makes baby strollers, which are sold in stores that carry other brands. The target audience is parents of babies. The assignment is to create an idea that showcases the superior comfort qualities of the client's stroller.

ELEVATOR PITCH: "You've asked us to promote your stroller's comfort qualities. That creates a very tough problem. The people who pay for strollers can't experience your product's superior comfort. And the people who can experience it can't talk—babies aren't able tell parents to choose *your* stroller. So what do we do? We turn parents into babies." (Then I would reveal the creative idea.) "We're going to build an adult-sized version of your stroller and give Mom and Dad in-store test rides."

Distill your points down to the bare minimum. Be brutal.

That's a very short setup, but look at how much heavy lifting it did. In twenty-two seconds, I established an almost insurmountable problem for which the agency then became a hero for solving. It made the creative idea much more impactful once revealed. I couldn't have done that without knowing ahead of time the two most important points I wanted to make. If you do the same thing before every presentation, you'll never be caught off guard when your audience is suddenly in a hurry. You'll still be able to show the work preceded by some good reasoning for why it's right for the assignment. Try it. Distill your points down to the bare minimum. Be brutal. When you're ready, grab a stopwatch and say the setup out loud. If your elevator pitch takes longer than thirty seconds, you're going to a floor that your audience doesn't have time for.

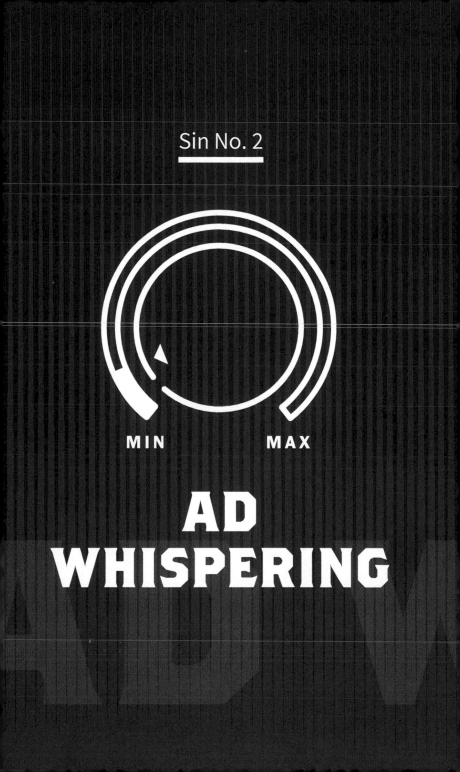

Sin No. 2

MIN   MAX

AD WHISPERING

✠

Ad Whispering is a catchall bucket that holds a bunch of mini sins. What they all have in common is stage presence. For the purposes of selling creative work, let's define a good presenter as someone who can capture an audience's attention, earn their trust quickly, and make them believers in the creative idea. Without stage presence, your ability to do these things is limited. The larger the audience, the more important stage presence becomes. But what if you don't have a big personality or aren't a naturally gifted orator? Can you still command a room? Sure. Just don't Ad Whisper.

Ad Whispering can manifest itself in a number of ways, but let's begin with what the name implies: volume. To command a room, you don't have to project your voice like Martin Luther King Jr. delivering his "I Have a Dream" speech, but you do have to register on a decibel meter. This is pretty basic, right? If someone in the back row keeps yelling, "speak up," it means the audience isn't hearing your idea. And when they can't hear it, they sure as hell won't buy it. Since this is a self-help book that cost you a few bucks, you're probably expecting me to provide a brilliant solution to the volume problem, so here it is: talk louder.

But don't talk to your shoes. Another form of Ad Whispering is looking down as you present or staring off at some imaginary object nobody else can see. If you're trying to build trust, this is definitely not the way to do it. As cliché as it may sound, eye contact is still the best way of connecting with an audience. And since you never know who has a vote in approving the work, make sure you visually connect with *everyone* in the room, not just the big boss. People who feel ignored are more likely to vote no than yes.

There's an even quicker way to disconnect from your audience than talking in hushed tones or gazing off into space. Turn your back on them. Ad Whisperers commit this sin all the time. Think about the physical layout of a typical presentation. The audience is in front of you and the screen is behind you. If you want to refer to something on the screen, you can do it only by turning around. That's okay as long as you turn back relatively soon. Unfortunately, many Ad Whisperers don't. Instead, they become slave to whatever is on the screen. It's not uncommon to see creative people say hello to the audience and then

KERRY Z. FEUERMAN

The fastest way to lose an audience is to turn your back on them.

turn their backs on them for the majority of their presentation, going through an entire campaign without visually reconnecting with the very people they hope will buy it. That's not exactly what I'd call a recipe for success. The best solution to this kind of Ad Whispering is to become thoroughly familiar with your presentation materials. Know the work so well that you could almost present it with no slides at all. Slides should be used as an accessory, not a crutch. When you're not chained to the screen, you'll become much more engaging.

You also need to be in control of what is on your slides. Most presentation decks aren't built by creative people. They're put together by people who are mainly concerned with logic flow and information, not presentation *style*. Which brings me to something I just have to get off my chest. Agencies: Stop using leave-behind decks as presentation decks! Your slides have way too much stuff on them. Bullet points, paragraphs of copy, multiple visuals, blah, blah, blah. Nothing kills a presenter's energy and spirit more, nothing makes a presenter as nervous and self-conscious, nothing creates a stilted, paint-by-numbers feeling in the room faster than reading a bunch of stuff off a screen. In fact, in those situations I'll argue that the presenter isn't even necessary. It's all on the slide. My advice is to create the leave-behind deck first, then ruthlessly hack away at it until it's a

Agencies: Stop using leave-behind decks as presentation decks!

short, punchy *presentation* deck. Give the client the leave-behind deck *after* the presentation!

Okay, I feel better. Let's move on.

Another crucial element of good stage presence is timing, the coordination and delivery of what you show with what you say. Ad Whisperers aren't very good at it. They don't realize that anything they put on a screen competes against them for people's attention. The instant you pull up a new slide, the audience's most dominant sense—sight—takes over. And since it's impossible for the brain to fully focus on two things at the same time, the audience simply stops listening. If what you're saying is key to understanding the idea, they may miss it entirely.

Timing is the secret weapon of all good presenters. They're masters of the reveal, not letting the audience see anything until they're ready for it to be seen. Good presenters study their presentation materials and pace them out for maximum impact. They click through individual frames instead of showing an entire storyboard all at once. They hold . . . hold . . . hold . . . bam! What sounds like a pretty good idea in the hands of a mediocre presenter *feels* like a great idea when presented by someone with deadly accurate timing. Basically, what I'm saying is this: if you want the audience to laugh out loud, don't show the punch line while you're still telling the joke.

Ad Whispering is the sin that keeps on sinning because people don't realize they're doing it. Self-awareness is a crucial part of being a good presenter. If you don't know you're mumbling or fidgeting around, how will you ever stop? But before you reach for the video camera, a word of caution: video is a double-edged sword. Watching yourself present can help you identify issues that need fixing, which is a good thing. On the other hand, video of your performance can make you so self-conscious that it leads to presentation paralysis, especially if you're a presenter who already lacks confidence. You end up worrying about every "um" you say, every move you make. I don't video people in my workshops because I think it can create more embarrassment than enlightenment. The better option is to ask someone you trust to tell you what you're doing wrong in a constructive way. Then make adjustments accordingly. Presenter, know thyself.

One last thing. Many presentations—most, in fact—don't take place in big rooms filled with a bunch of clients. They happen in cramped little offices with creative directors, planners, and account people. Tons of ideas are pinned to the wall, feet are on the table, alcohol is probably involved if it's after six. In other words, they don't *feel* like moments where stage presence matters. But they are. At least, for good presenters they are. Whenever you present an idea, whether you're sitting down or standing up, you're on stage. A more casual stage in many cases, but a stage nonetheless, where the fate of your work can depend on how well you bring it to life. When all things are equal, when your work and another team's work are both good, the person who paints a more vivid picture and makes a smarter argument is more likely to be successful. That is to say, the best actors on stage win.

Whether you're sitting down or standing up, you're on stage.

Sin No. 3

WANDERLUST

✠

Why did the chicken cross the road? To get to the other side.

Now imagine if the joke were told like this: *Why did the brown-and-white chicken with short legs and a worm in its mouth cross the road filled with lots of really deep, randomly spaced potholes? To get to the other side, the shady side, which was at least fifty—no, make that sixty—feet away.*

You have just experienced Wanderlust, the most common deadly sin out there. Wanderlust is a whole lot of talking that usually says very little and basically leads nowhere valuable. Or if it does make a point, you can't find it because there's so much irrelevant, unnecessary language surrounding it. We all know Wanderlusters in our personal lives, right? They're the people who start a story that goes on and on. They never quite finish it but begin another, often unrelated story without so much as taking a breath. I swear, the word "non sequitur" was invented for these folks. Sometimes they can be charming, even endearing in their compassless monologues. But most of the time when Wanderlusters speak, I simply check out. That is, I stop listening to them, which is exactly what a client does when a presentation isn't focused and clear.

So why do so many presenters commit Wanderlust? I believe it comes down to three things:

1. **Nervousness**
2. **Poor preparation**
3. **No plan**

If you've ever felt as if your heart were going to beat out of your chest, or wished you'd doubled your antiperspirant before standing up to present, you've experienced some of the physical effects that nervousness can cause. Uncomfortable, to be sure, but these usually aren't presentation killers. For that, you need to experience the kind of nervousness that seriously impacts your *mental* state. In medical terms, your mind turns to mush. It might be your first new business pitch or an internal creative review with senior agency people. You stand up to speak and suddenly draw a blank. And so you just start talking—*wandering*. If you're lucky, it's not too obvious to your audience, and slowly you regain your train of thought. But I don't have

You stand up to speak and suddenly draw a blank.

fig. 3

OVERCOME NERVOUSNESS

THE FIVE DEADLY SINS OF PRESENTING CREATIVE WORK

This golfer releases tension by waggling the club before he swings.
Nervous presenters should have their own version of a waggle.

much faith in luck, especially when good work is at stake. So I have a strategy for overcoming nervousness before it can grip me by the throat. It's called the "waggle."

One of the greatest golfers of all time was a man named Ben Hogan. One day Ben realized that as he stood over the ball and prepared to swing, his muscles began to tighten up. The more time he took, the more tense he became. As any golfer will tell you, tension is the enemy of a well-executed golf swing. So Ben invented the waggle. Just before starting his backswing, he gave the club a small shake back and forth. That little action with his hands had the effect of relaxing his entire body—and mind. The resulting swing was a thing of beauty.

When you think about it, presenting creative work isn't all that different from swinging a golf club. Waiting for your turn to present is like standing over the ball. You start to get nervous, which leads to your muscles tightening and your brain slowly seizing up. If you don't release this tension with some sort of waggle, you'll have a much harder time getting into the groove of your presentation (swinging smoothly). So what will your waggle be? Chances are, you won't have a golf club with you, so come up with something else. Open a water bottle and take a sip. Roll up your shirtsleeves as you walk to the front of the room. Take off your jacket. Make a self-effacing joke. Comment on the weather. Tell a short (but relevant) story. I don't care what you do, just so long as you have a waggle in your back pocket in case you need it, something that gets you out of presentation paralysis. Just knowing that it's there can sometimes be enough to keep nervousness down to a manageable level. As those Harvard psychologists showed us, the beginning of a presentation is when the audience decides whether they trust you and whether they think you're good at what you do. Start strong and nothing can stop you.

Unless you didn't prepare. *Really* prepare.

Poor preparation is a self-inflicted wound that's nearly impossible to recover from. Once you realize how unprepared you are, you're already into the presentation. With each new concept you bumble through, things just get worse and worse. Wanderlusters try to blab their way out of it. But that's like a pilot in a death spiral pulling back harder and harder on the control stick, making the plane spin even faster until it plows into the ground.

This rarely happens to good presenters. They always prepare. The first thing they do is review the creative brief, making sure they understand the client's ask. Next, they go through each piece of creative

Poor preparation is a self-inflicted wound that's nearly impossible to recover from.

work—especially if they didn't create it—familiarizing themselves with all of the executional elements. When there's copy involved, they read it and read it again. If it's a multimedia campaign, they study how all the pieces work as a whole. Only then do they organize their materials into a presentation that has a natural flow, a flow that ties everything together into a neat, irresistible package. You'd think they'd be done at this point, but not quite. Smart presenters take control of their portion of the deck, building their own slides in a way that's comfortable for their personal presentation style. Unnecessary slides are weeded out. All temptations to Wanderlust are removed. Basically, good presenters are control freaks.

Okay, now let's talk about having a plan—and how it's different from preparing for the presentation. Preparation is all about the actions you're going to take in the presentation itself. It's tactical, executional. A plan, on the other hand, looks at everything from thirty thousand feet. It's strategic. In the real world of everyday advertising, not all presentations have or really need to have a strategic plan. It's the biggies that do—major campaigns, new business pitches. This is when the triumvirate of account person, planner, and creative person put their heads together and build a coordinated, almost military-style attack: Should we create a mood video (air cover)? How will the account person presell the client (soften the beaches)? What questions should we anticipate (defensive positions)? Now that's building a plan. If you're a junior creative person, this is above your pay grade, but that doesn't mean you shouldn't pay attention. The better you get at presenting, the faster you'll be asked to join these kinds of strategic meetings. That's when your career will launch to the next level.

While I always believe in taking the offensive, let me relate a story where the plan relied entirely on defense: stopping an onslaught of tough client questions. Several years ago, The Martin Agency was pitching Quiznos restaurants. When it came time for me to present the work, I didn't start with TV or digital or any work at all. The campaign I was about to show was so bizarre that without a preemptive defensive move, we would have been overrun by shell-shocked clients. The solution came in the form of a target-audience video.

At the time, Quiznos' main target was males eighteen to twenty-four years old. They're not like normal people. They jump off balconies into swimming pools. They use the phrase "Hey, watch this" a lot. They're, well, you know, *guys*. So a week before the pitch, the agency set out to find some at a local university. We intercepted our targets on their way to class and asked if they'd put on some headphones and watch something on a laptop (animated rodents singing a song about

Quiznos subs) while we videoed them. Without the camera seeing what was on the laptop, we pushed Play . . . and they started laughing. And hooting. And loving. And wanting more. We cut together a video of their reactions and played it for the Quiznos clients during the pitch, with no explanation whatsoever. When it was done I said to them, "What are those guys looking at? Oh wait, I know. Your new campaign." We hit the Play button one more time so the clients could see the rodents (officially called Spongmonkeys) for themselves. After recovering from the shock, they agreed that what looked like gross, repugnant, ugly little creatures to them were actually lovable, hilarious, cool characters to their target audience. The plan to preempt their reactions worked. We won.

Unfortunately, the Quiznos story is a rarity. Too many presentations are created by multiple people working in their own individual silos, then slapped together at the last minute with no coordinated plan for selling the work. The account person presents his business part. The planner does her strategic part. Then the creative team puts on their show, often neglecting everything their fellow presenters just said. This is a formula for group Wanderlust, three separate presentations masquerading as one. And what's lost is the ability to build *cumulative* impact. I don't care if you're the most junior person on the team; ask your account and planning partners to work with you on a

Too many presentations are created by multiple people working in their own individual silos, then slapped together at the last minute.

plan for selling the work. Go in with arms locked. Or at least holding hands.

The excuse for poor preparation or not having a plan is always the same: no time. I don't buy that. There's always time. Whether you review the finished deck at 2:00 a.m. or come up with your opening statement while showering the morning of the presentation, there's time. A plan can be hatched by team members in the taxi on the way to the meeting. Roles can be discussed for supporting the work in ten minutes. Questions anticipated in five. There's always, always time. You just have to make a choice: Will you use it to get ready for the presentation? Or will you use it after the presentation to reconcept?

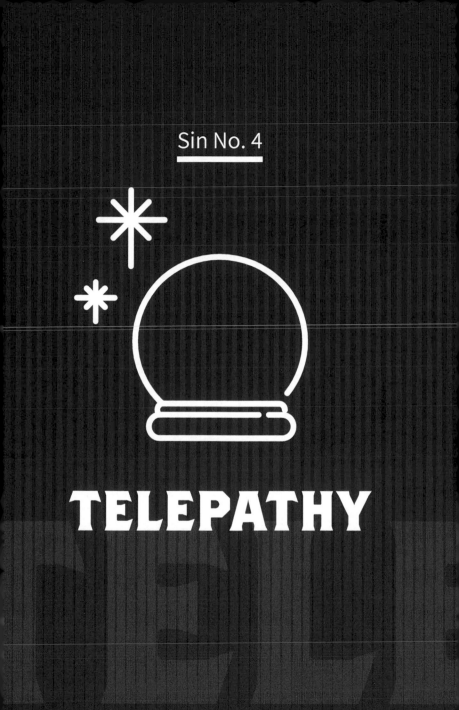

Sin No. 4

TELEPATHY

✠

The opposite of Wanderlust, yet equally bad, is a presentation that leaves out crucial information. For an industry that's supposed to be about communicating, too many concepts die simply because the presenters don't explain them very well—don't connect the dots. Clients aren't mind readers. If they have to ask a bunch of questions just to get the idea, it makes them wonder if consumers won't get it, either.

Strange as it may sound, Telepathy is often caused by presenters being excited about the work. Once they get on a roll, they start to talk faster and faster, hands flying, crucial little pieces of information being left out along the way. Enthusiasm takes over at the expense of clarity. The truth is, you have to be enthusiastic and clear simultaneously. Walk and chew gum at the same time, as they say. For that, I suggest doing two things. First, assume the audience knows absolutely nothing. Think of them as art critics looking at a totally blank

First, assume the audience knows absolutely nothing.

canvas on which you must paint a vivid picture of the idea. Second, limit your intake of Red Bull.

By the time creative work reaches a client presentation, it's probably gone through several presentations within the agency. As the presenter, you might be so familiar with the work you could recite it in your sleep. It's hard to remember that clients are going to be seeing it for the very first time. All the stuff speeding through your brain isn't in theirs. Which means you have to back up, take the clients by the hand, and bring them up to your level of understanding before they're able to fairly pass judgment on the work. Again, this requires smart preparation. Before the presentation, ask yourself this: What do they need to know in order to understand the idea? Then wrap the answer in enthusiasm and let the show begin.

I was sort of joking about the Red Bull thing, but not entirely. If you have a naturally energetic personality, you should know that there's a tipping point where it can become overwhelming to your audience, particularly when it's a small group. I've seen presenters verbally connect the dots only to have the information lost in a hurricane of presentation hyperactivity. Bigger isn't always better. Good presenters are able to dial up or dial down their performance depending on the

COMMUNICATE CLEARLY

fig. 4

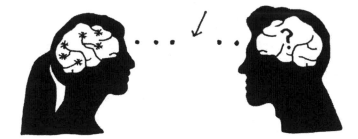

THE FIVE DEADLY SINS OF PRESENTING CREATIVE WORK

If you don't connect the dots, don't expect your audience to understand the idea.

size and nature of the audience. They know that *how* you present is often as important as *what* you present.

This can even apply to your physical presence, as it did to me several years ago. I was freelancing for a shop in New York when, after selling a campaign internally, they asked me to present to the client's new chief marketing officer in person. Just before the meeting began, I asked the account supervisor what the new CMO was like. Her reply: "He thinks he's the king and agency people are his subjects." Wow. On the spot I made the decision to change my presentation style from big to small. I decided that instead of standing and presenting at a level *above* the CMO, I would sit *across* from him and act more deferential (subject to king) while showing the campaign. If catering to this guy's grandiose personality was going to help sell the work, I figured that was the smart thing to do. As it turned out, I wasn't wrong. Smaller was better. It was a textbook example of avoiding what I call "emotional telepathy": information being lost because your audience doesn't *want* to listen very hard.

Telepathy is the easiest sin to commit but it can also be the easiest to fix. It's simply a matter of taking what's inside your head and putting it inside the heads of your audience. Start with the big picture—or as I like to say, the house. The house is the overarching idea. Once the audience understands that, you can fill in all the rooms you want: TV executions, social media tie-ins, events, content films, and so on. This means you have to be able to articulate the big idea clearly and concisely. If you can't, you're not ready to make the presentation. I used to take a piece of paper and write out the big idea until I could get it down to a single brief sentence. I'd hand it to someone not involved with the project and ask if they understood the idea. If they didn't, I kept refining the sentence until they did.

As you fill in the rooms of the house, remember, clients don't think and talk the way creative people do. I've presented to chief marketing officers who had zero background in marketing or advertising. They were sales or tech people being groomed to one day run the company, so they ran different divisions for a year or two to learn them all. Even mid- and lower-level clients who've majored in communications don't absorb creative ideas as quickly as those of us who make them for a living. They're not dumb, by any means. It's just that we speak in creative shorthand, just as musicians, surgeons, pilots, or any other specialized group of people communicate among themselves. If you have a complicated execution to present—one with narration, dialogue, supers, multiple scenes, freeze-frames, etc.—take your time and make sure the audience is following along. On the other hand, don't overexplain it. There's a difference between connecting the dots and having too many dots. You'll lose your audience in the weeds. Like most things, presenting creative ideas is a balancing act between too little and too much.

One of the ways good presenters avoid committing Telepathy is by periodically checking in with the audience. They take a little pause and ask if everyone is clear on the idea. If they suspect someone isn't 100 percent following along, they'll say, "Just in case, I'll do a quick recap," and give a condensed version of the idea. It also never hurts to have a good wingman looking out for you. Account people can act as excellent early-warning radar systems in a presentation. While you're going Mach 2 with your hair on fire, they can scan the room in search of subtle signs that the audience isn't following along and deftly chime in with any missing pieces. This, of course, requires a good deal of trust between you and your account team (a book in itself). If your wingman is going to interrupt your flow, you have to believe it's for the good of selling the work. This I learned just before starting my first job in advertising. My brother had been a copywriter for several years before me, so I asked him if he had any advice. He said, "Yeah. Find yourself a good account person and hold on to him for dear life because he's worth his weight in gold." I said, "Aren't you going to tell me something about creative work?" He replied, "I just did."

One deadly sin
can easily lead
to another.

One last thing to keep in mind: be aware that during a presentation, one deadly sin can easily lead to another. Take Telepathy and Wanderlust, for example. When a presenter leaves out important information, the audience becomes confused, even lost. Inevitably, someone will raise a hand and start asking questions, and you'll have no choice but to answer them. Good presenters give the answer and then immediately get back on the highway to where the presentation is headed. They know that the fastest way to get from point A (assignment) to point B (creative solution) is a straight line. When undisciplined presenters stop to answer questions, however, they can have a hard time picking back up where the presentation left off. They spend precious minutes Wanderlusting. Eventually, they may get back on the highway, but by then the momentum has been lost. This is why following a well-organized deck is so important. It's a road map that keeps you from driving aimlessly around back roads. Or worse, over a cliff.

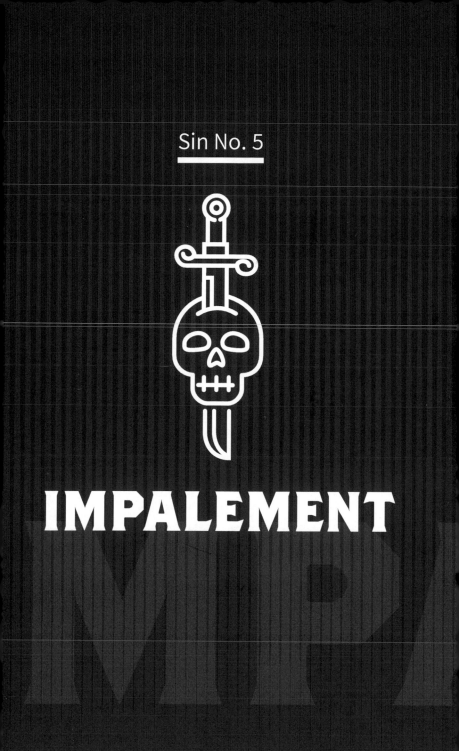

IMPALEMENT

If you played Whac-A-Mole as a kid, you'll be happy to know that your time wasn't wasted. It was a perfect training ground for the final phase of every presentation: Q&A. Knowing how to defend creative work against a barrage of tough (okay, sometimes dumb) questions is as important as being able to present it in the first place. Good presenters stay calm and deftly maneuver their way through this game of wits. The minute a question pops up, they neutralize it with thoughtfulness and tact. In fact, I used to welcome this part of the presentation, preferring to get issues on the table right then and there, while the top client was still in the meeting. Without a bodyguard in the room to defend it, creative work is vulnerable to all sorts of probing and challenges, both fair and unfair. But remember, there's a difference between defending ideas and being *defensive*. A defensive response can make a client wonder what your motivation is: Solving their business needs or padding your portfolio?

I believe that good clients want their agencies to fight for creative work. They understand passion. They appreciate a solid rebuttal. Some are even willing to entertain a presentation of work they've already rejected. So push it as far as you can. But there comes a point when you have to recognize the warning signs of when a fight is lost. It starts with subtle body language, like a tightening jaw muscle. That progresses to the more obvious visual cues: pursing of the lips, crossing of the arms, a firm shaking of the head. If you miss those red flags, the client turns to the account people and gives them *The Look*. Even a blind man can't miss *The Look*. It means that you're committing the sin of Impalement. And if you fall on your sword any harder, the work won't be the only thing that dies. Smart presenters live to fight another day.

Committing Impalement is as old as advertising itself. When you've put your heart and soul into creating work—work you truly believe in—it's extremely difficult to let it die. When you're presenting concepts created by people other than yourself, it's even harder because they expect you to fight your ass off for it. So how do you do that without hurting your relationship with the client? Well, let me tell you first what you don't do: box. Don't try to go toe to toe with the client. You will rarely win this way because clients are always in a higher weight class than you. They control the money and have final

Smart presenters live to fight another day.

approval of the work. Or, to keep the analogy going, they have a longer reach and a more powerful punch. If you want to win, definitely don't box. Instead, use judo.

Judo is the art of using your opponent's energy to your advantage. If a big screaming guy runs at you with raised fists and you know judo, you don't stand there and hold your ground. Instead, you step aside just before the crash, grab him by the lapels, and use his momentum to flip him over your back and onto the floor. Hopefully you won't ever have to literally do that with a client. But when a big, tough question comes hurtling your way, flipping it to serve your purposes can be a very effective thing.

Here's an example of presentation judo.

SITUATION: You've just presented a brilliant digital campaign that uses celebrities. The client says she loves the campaign but doesn't want to spend the money on celebrities. She thinks the idea works just as well using normal people.

You're the creative director. Which response would you give?

1.   I don't agree. That will ruin the idea.

fig. 5

HANDLE TOUGH QUESTIONS

Defend ideas like this and you will lose.

Defend ideas like this and you might win.

2. Okay, we'll get rid of the celebrities.

3. You know, I had the exact same thought when the team showed me the idea. Do we really need celebs? The team pointed out something I hadn't thought of: Twitter. The combined Twitter following of our celebrities is over twenty million people. That's a lot of free media.

If you chose response number three, congratulations. You are now a judo black belt. You could have just said that celebrities have huge Twitter followings, a pretty good answer on its own since few clients can resist free media. But that would have been simply stating a fact. The real power in your answer was that *you* were also skeptical of the need for celebrities. You were smart enough to share this, and as a result you and the client became birds of a feather. A simpatico bond was formed that put you in a better position to persuade (judo) rather than argue (box).

Falling on your sword for creative work might make you a temporary hero inside the creative department, but how much help will you be in selling future campaigns if you've been asked off the account? That happened to me twice in my career, and I'm not proud of either time.

Looking back, I now realize why it happened. I was still in the bull-headed phase of my creative director evolution, beyond Neanderthal but not quite *Homo sapiens*. It took me years to learn that the best creative people figure out how to save an idea without diminishing it or damaging their relationship with the client. They become good *negotiators*.

Negotiation isn't limited to the actual presentation of an idea. It can be equally important in protecting and producing work that's already been sold. I remember my first big test in having to negotiate on the fly. Naturally, it took place in Nome, Alaska, temperature twenty-four below zero. We had come to Nome to shoot a campaign for Eskimo Pie. The director was atop a huge crane with his DP, setting up an epic shot of the frozen Bering Sea when the client, clad in full arctic attire, waddled up to me. He looked like a penguin with a problem. "I want to change the shot," he said. Alarm bells went off in my head. *We have to stop this madman!* (Actually, he was a nice guy, but nice guys don't make for good stories.) So I suggested we take a walk and have a chat. By the time we returned, the shot was all set up and the client was on board . . . as long as we shot an *alternate*. The final decision would be made in an editing suite in California. We hadn't won yet, but we hadn't lost, either. Six months later, Eskimo Pie brand awareness was up and, as a sweet bonus, the agency collected a silver medal for the campaign at The One Show. In case you're wondering, the original shot stayed in.

The best negotiators choose their battles and battlefields wisely. Had I opted to argue my case right there in front of the whole crew, I would have paid for it down the road. I knew the argument I was making was right, but being right isn't always enough. In fact, it can be downright dangerous. If you don't handle the issue with a deft touch, you end up proving that your client (or boss) is wrong. As your career counselor here, let me use an excerpt from a book called *The Pillars of the Earth* by Ken Follett to make the point. In medieval England, a priest is planning to fight the king on a contentious issue involving the church. And he thinks he can beat the king. But a fellow priest wisely encourages him to tread lightly, warning, "A man who loses a battle with his king may be forgiven. But a man who wins such a battle is doomed."

Okay, let's do some more role-playing.

SITUATION: You're the creative director. A week after getting a commercial approved, you receive a call from a very upset client saying he saw a spot just like it on TV last night. You tell him you'll call back in fifteen minutes, hang up, and go straight to

The best negotiators choose their battles and battlefields wisely.

YouTube. The only thing in the commercial that's even remotely the same as yours is a goat. When you try to call the client back, he's so pissed off he won't answer the phone.

You decide to (pick one):

1. Ask the account person to call the client.
2. Show both commercials to a quickly assembled group of consumers, video their reactions, and send a link to the client.
3. Email the client saying there have been dozens of commercials with goats and he shouldn't worry about it. Yours is funnier.

For those who chose option two, I applaud your initiative. But I don't agree. This is a situation where being right isn't enough. There is absolutely no way this furious client is going to listen to reason—from you, the account person, or anyone. All he sees is a copycat commercial (technically, a copygoat commercial). You're much better off letting the situation defuse itself or, if you have to, developing a new spot overnight. Unlike the client in the Eskimo Pie example, this client is in no mood to negotiate a compromise. Arguing that the spots are different from one another will simply make him question your *judgment*, which is a wound that very rarely heals and frequently turns gangrenous. Don't fall on your sword. If you have to kill something, kill the goat.

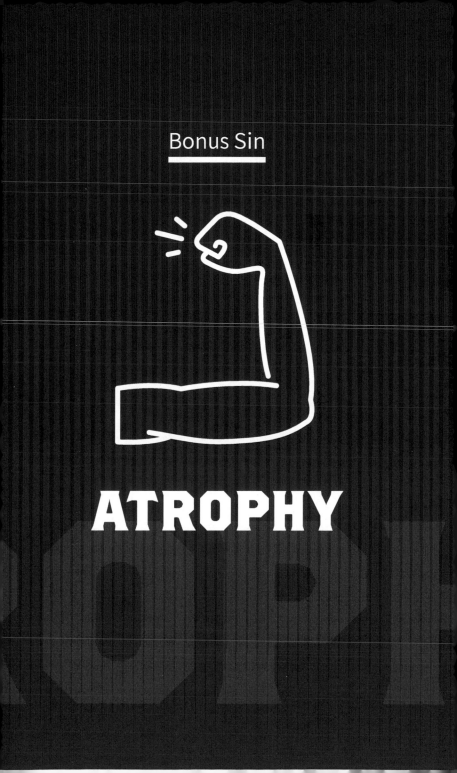

ATROPHY

✟

At the beginning of this survival guide, I mentioned Pope Gregory and the original seven deadly sins. Apparently, the pontiff was concerned that simply telling people sinning was bad wasn't going to keep them from doing it. But tell them that if they sinned, they'd get stoned to death by their neighbors and spend eternity roasting in the flames of hell . . . well, now you've got their attention.

Here's what concerns me: you'll think about the five deadly sins of presenting creative work only when you have a big presentation coming up. That's a mistake. Presentation skills are like a muscle. The more you exercise it, the more powerful you will become. But let that muscle go unused for any length of time and it will atrophy. Work that might have lived had you maintained your skills is less likely to survive. That may not be as painful as getting hit in the head with a rock, but it will still hurt. And it won't hurt just you—it will hurt the agency. And, assuming the work is good, possibly the client's business.

The absolute last thing you want to do is avoid making presentations.

I'm *always* in presentation mode, be it during an internal review with account people and planners or when showing a bunch of tissue concepts to a creative director. Or even when convincing my art director partner to like a concept. When I want someone—anyone—to support an idea, I flex my presentation skills muscle. It's usually pretty subtle. In fact, it doesn't feel like I'm presenting at all. I'm "sharing." Or "showing." Or "asking" for an opinion. Call it what you want. What's important is that I'm *thinking* like a presenter, figuring out what my audience needs to hear in order to buy into the idea. I keep it clear and simple. I stay focused and connect the dots. All I care about is getting agreement to move on to the next person in the approval process (of which there are usually too many).

I can't tell you how many times I've heard people say they don't like to present because they're not good at it. If that isn't a self-fulfilling prophecy, I don't know what is. The absolute last thing you want to do is avoid making presentations. Other than creating great work, having the ability to stand up and sell it is the most important skill set you can develop. I'm not saying it's going to be easy. I'm not suggesting you won't get nervous—you will. In fact, the best presenter I've ever known used to throw up before every big presentation. That is, until he got good at making them. With enough practice, fear of presenting will be replaced by a feeling of power. Ask any great presenter what it feels like to command a room, and they'll tell you it's a natural high, a drug that's hard to get enough of. If you need any more motivation than that, how does money sound? Great presenters give agencies an edge in all sorts of situations, not the least of which are new business pitches. It's an edge that agencies are all too happy to pay handsomely for because when everything else is equal, the presenter is the tiebreaker. *Cha-ching*.

Of course, there will be times when even the world's greatest presenter won't be able to sell a creative idea. All the charm, smarts, stage presence, and Q&A dexterity won't persuade an audience that doesn't want to be sold. The problem is, you never know when those situations will occur. It reminds me of the famous quote by John Wanamaker, a prominent businessman in late-nineteenth-century Philadelphia, who said, "Half the money I spend on advertising is wasted; the trouble is, I don't know which half." So, too, for selling creativity. Here's how I look at it: There's a certain amount of work, let's say 25 percent, that sits on a fence. It could fall either way depending on who's showing it. Your job as a presenter is to nudge it off the fence into the "sold" side. Which 25 percent will it be? You'll never know. That's why you can't let your skills atrophy.

fig. 6

BREAK THE TIE

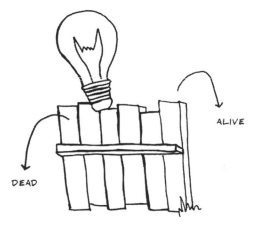

ALIVE

DEAD

A lot of creative ideas sit on a fence in the client's mind.
Good presenters provide a gentle nudge.

Like all creative people, I have a win/loss record: work living versus work dying. My presentations usually fell into one of two categories: being in The Zone or having an Out of Body Experience. The Zone is pretty self-explanatory, so let's talk about the other one, the bad one. My Out of Body Experiences were exactly what they sound like, me watching me. I felt as if I were literally standing outside my body observing myself do a poor job. Everything moved in slow motion, nothing I said was any good. If you've ever had a dream where something bad is happening but you're powerless to do anything about it, then you know what I'm talking about. Fortunately, my OBEs didn't occur very often, and over time I began to recognize what was at the root of them. My skills had atrophied. It had been months between formal presentations, and I had simply fallen into the old habit of winging it. By realizing this and treating even little creative reviews as mini presentations, I kept my muscle strong. The OBEs went away forever.

THERE'S NO SIN IN BEING YOU

✝

Early in my career I was lucky to work with a handful of excellent presenters, and I learned something different from all of them. The single most important thing I learned was this: I'm not them. And I shouldn't try to be them. The biggest mistake you can make as a presenter is to try to be someone you're not.

My first creative director was six foot four, *GQ* handsome, wore a double-breasted suit as if he were born in it, had a voice made for movie trailers, and was dripping with charisma, not to mention smarts. There was no way I could have presented like him, starting with the fact that I'm five foot eight on a tall day. So instead, I went with a style that played to *my* strengths—directness, humor, storytelling. It's been successful for me not because I worked at it but rather because I didn't have to work at it. It is *who I am*. There are plenty of effective presentation styles: big/animated, quiet/thoughtful, smart/no bullshit, crazy like a fox/funny. Whether you know it or not, you've

Don't try to be someone you're not built to be.

been developing your style since the day you were born. The trick is to realize what that style is, embrace it, and don't try to be someone you're not built to be. Judy Garland said it best: "Always be a first-rate version of yourself, instead of a second-rate version of somebody else."

Knowing who you are is a good start. But that's all it is, a start. If you want to rise above your fellow creatives or kick the asses of competing creative directors, you'll need to build on that foundation. There's no faster way to do that than by adding a few force multipliers. Force multiplier is a military term that refers to anything that makes you more effective. For a soldier, that can be as simple as attaching a grenade launcher to his rifle. Nothing else changes, he's the exact same soldier, only now he's more powerful on the battlefield. There are all sorts of force multipliers available to presenters: knowledge, quotes, props, facts and figures, storytelling, etc. By judiciously adding them to a presentation, you can become more engaging and persuasive without changing your personal style one bit.

Example: When I'm doing a presentation skills workshop with senior-level people, I often start by putting up this quote from Winston Churchill: "I am always ready to learn, although I do not always like being taught." It's my way of showing respect to the audience, essentially saying, *I know that you're experienced people. I'm not here to school you. I'm here to share with you.* Shown alongside a picture of Sir Winston scowling at the camera, the quote gets a laugh and addresses the elephant in the room: they've already made plenty of presentations in their careers. Instantly, I've multiplied my effectiveness with this group for the rest of the class.

Props can be very powerful force multipliers. Let's say you're about to present a digital campaign that targets an extremely small, elusive audience. The concept is very edgy and cool. The clients are less so. Here's how you can use a prop to make a stronger case for the work: Take a four-by-eight-foot piece of white foam board and put it against a wall before the meeting. As you start to present, grab a red marker and draw a small X in the middle of the foam board, then say, "As you know, we're targeting a tiny group of people." Walk twenty feet back from the foam board and take a dart out of your pocket. Throw it at the X. Then throw two more darts. Chances are, you'll miss the X entirely, at which point you say, "The odds of hitting such a small audience are pretty slim. So what if we did the exact opposite? What if we aimed at a *larger* audience instead? What if we posted a video that was so insanely funny people would share it on social media with all their friends, *including* our target?" That's when you show the idea. By metaphorically demonstrating the problem, you've magnified the business challenge facing the client. Maybe, just maybe, they'll now

MULTIPLY YOUR EFFECTIVENESS

fig. 7

"NEVER INTERRUPT YOUR ENEMY WHILE HE IS MAKING A MISTAKE."

– NAPOLEON

This mild-mannered presenter uses a quote to add power to the point she's making.

consider an idea that goes beyond their normal comfort zone. One thing is for damn sure, they'll never forget your presentation.

I employed all sorts of props throughout my career. When presenting to a large publicly traded company, I once used my cell phone to pull up the company's stock price on the New York Stock Exchange. I held up a photograph of a little girl while reading a note she wrote in crayon from her hospital bed. I took a can of beer and popped the tab, letting the unmistakable sound hang in the air. I'll admit that occasionally my props were a bit theatrical, like the dart-throwing example, but most of the time they were pretty understated. But effective.

If you want to see a good example of someone using simple props to pull in an audience, go to YouTube and type in "Simon Sinek: how great leaders inspire action." Sinek uses a black marker to draw what he calls the "Golden Circle" on a white easel pad. He could have shown a slick, well-designed graphic of the Golden Circle on a big flat screen instead, but that wouldn't have been nearly as engaging. Sinek's *drawing* of three rings and then labeling of each one creates a gradual, more intriguing reveal of his idea. The combination of a well-delivered voice-over with low-tech props is irresistible to his audience.

What about knowledge? How can you use that as a force multiplier? Well, it's as simple as knowing something your audience doesn't and sharing it in an interesting, meaningful way. Let's stay with Simon Sinek's presentation for a minute. The subject of his talk is how good leaders inspire action. Early in the talk he brings up an interesting fact about the Wright brothers: neither Wilbur nor Orville had college educations, yet they still managed to beat well-educated, more qualified, better-financed competitors in the race for powered flight. He uses that interesting piece of history to explain why companies with strong belief systems (the Wright brothers believed they could change the world) inspire employees and consumers more than companies that simply make products (Orville and Wilbur's competitors were motivated by making money). Knowledge is power, as the saying goes. Presenters like Simon Sinek know how to use it to sell their ideas.

Storytelling. It's a bit of an overused buzzword these days, but that aside, it's still a useful force multiplier. In fact, storytelling may be the most effective way to engage an audience quickly, moving them from sitting back in their chairs to leaning forward. There are all kinds of storytelling, of course, but I'm going to focus on only one: how you got to the creative idea you're about to present. Clients rarely know how hard agencies work on their behalf, so tell it as a story. Use the journey of creative discovery to build a little anticipation (and maybe some appreciation) before showing the work. A friend of mine did that very thing several years ago. Here's what he said to the clients before unveiling a campaign. "When we first saw this assignment, everyone loved it. That lasted about three days. I can't tell you exactly why, but no one could crack it. We must have looked at a hundred ideas. A lot of them were okay, some were even pretty good. But nothing was great. Anyway, by Saturday night we were all burned out, so I went home, fell into bed, and was instantly dead to the world. At two a.m. my phone rang. 'Hello?' It was one of the creative teams. I said in a groggy voice, 'This better be fucking worth it.' Well, it was." With that little peek behind the curtain, the clients were primed and excited to see something special from their hardworking agency. Storytelling created *anticipation*, a tasty appetizer leading to the big meal.

Every force multiplier I just talked about was easy to come up with. In fact, it took me less than five minutes to find that quote by Winston Churchill. You can do the exact same thing—if you bother to think about it. Once you get your presentation organized, look at it and ask yourself the one question all great presenters ask: "How can I make this more *interesting*?"

Ask yourself the one question all great presenters ask: "How can I make this more interesting?"

I want to leave you by debunking a myth. A lot of people believe that being a great presenter is a *gift*, a talent you're either born with or you're not. That ridiculous notion needs a dagger plunged into its heart right here and now. Sure, there are naturally magnetic personalities at almost every agency, people with more charisma than seems fair to the rest of us. But that's just a small piece of what it takes to persuade an audience to buy what you're selling, especially when a lot of dough is on the line. Every great presenter I've ever known will tell you the real truth: they work at it. They do everything discussed in the preceding pages and then some. They know their own strengths, and they play to them. They know their client's business problem. They prepare a smart argument for the work. They organize their materials and simplify their slides. They build their deck for impact, not just information. They anticipate questions and issues. And they review it all, over and over again. Only then do they relax.

That's when the magic happens.

NOTES

ABOUT THE AUTHOR

Kerry Feuerman's professional life began as a helicopter pilot. That didn't seem dangerous enough, so he switched to advertising. As a global creative director, he presented to audiences around the world, selling creative work that has run in more than forty countries. Feuerman's long list of blue-chip clients has included Mercedes-Benz, Saab, the US Army, Citi, Seiko, and Infiniti. In 2015, he began his own company, Last Hurdle, and now conducts presentation workshops focused on selling creative ideas. Visit his website, lasthurdle.net, for workshop information.

Made in the USA
Middletown, DE
21 November 2018